Series Editor: Catherine Bow

The **Faith in Action** Series

Story of the 14th Dalai Lama

Andrew Ahmed and Vanessa Gray

Illustrated by Brian Platt

RELIGIOUS AND MORAL EDUCATION PRESS

EXILED LEADER

The Story of the 14th Dalai Lama

C ymbals crashed together in the otherwise quiet room as the young Dalai Lama glanced round the shrine for the last time. He felt sick and afraid, but putting a silk scarf before the statue of his ferocious-looking protector god made him feel a little better. The other Buddhist monks sensed a change in the air. Bowing their heads, they continued their prayers. Part of the Dalai Lama knew he might never see the Potala Palace, his home for nearly twenty years, again. Danger from Chinese soldiers was driving him from his country of Tibet.

The young man walked around the huge Potala Palace in Lhasa (the capital of Tibet) for the last time before putting on his disguise. Wearing the stiff heavy overcoat and fur hat of a Tibetan guardsman felt strange to him, as he had worn only monk's robes since the age of five. Even more disturbing was the need to carry a rifle – a lethal weapon. He went alone into his prayer room and sat on his beautiful gold and red throne. Looking through a book of the Buddha's teachings he found a passage where the Buddha advised his followers to be brave. The Dalai Lama tried to draw strength from this.

His mother, sister and thirteen-year-old brother, together with some attendants, had slipped out of

the city after darkness had fallen. The Dalai Lama followed half an hour later, at ten o'clock. There was no moon, but on the 'roof of the world' on that cloudless night in March 1959, the stars were clear and bright. The Dalai Lama was very nervous as he groped his way across the dark, silent park to his bodyguard, who waited armed with a sword. He held his breath as they walked through the outer gates past groups of Tibetans, afraid that someone would recognize him and the escape would fail. The bodyguard called out to the Chinese soldiers that they were on a routine tour of inspection then suddenly they were out in the open and vulnerable.

The Dalai Lama had been told not to wear his glasses as they might cause him to be recognized, but this was hopeless. Without them, he just stumbled around in the darkness. After struggling over a river which had to be crossed on stepping-stones he decided it was less of a risk to put them on.

They soon arrived at the rendezvous point where his family were waiting, and the dangerous trek across the Himalayan Mountains began. In the confusion of the hasty escape some very important monks found themselves astride gold jewelled saddles weighing down shaggy little mules, whilst young novices (trainee monks) sitting on rags rode high up on powerful stallions. With his spectacles on the Dalai Lama saw torches and fires blazing only 300 metres away. He realized the party was creeping past a camp of Chinese soldiers. He hardly dared to breathe for fear of being heard.

More Tibetans who had sneaked away from Lhasa and other towns under the noses of the Chinese army met up with the Dalai Lama's group. In addition there were over three hundred Tibetan soldiers who vowed to protect their young leader, making almost five hundred people altogether. Somehow this huge group had to remain undetected and reach the border before the Chinese caught up with them. Everyone was heavily armed. Even the Dalai Lama's personal cook carried a huge bazooka (a hand-held rocket launcher) despite not knowing how to fire or reload it. They all prayed the weapons would not be needed.

Back in Lhasa the Chinese army was already bombing temples and monasteries, and machine-gunning people in the streets. Even high up in the mountain passes the party did not dare slacken its pace as an aeroplane whined above, searching for them. Some could not keep up and turned back. The Dalai Lama never learnt what happened to them.

Towards the end of the seventeen-day journey terrible blizzards raged and exhaustion was pushing them to breaking point. On the last night, freezing rain poured into the Dalai Lama's tent, and no matter where he dragged his bedding the water soon soaked into it. The next day fever raged through his body leaving him too ill to move on. He spent the day sleeping in a cow shed until he was strong enough to lead his weary party out of Tibet and into India – to freedom.

What Do You Think?

Important: In answering 'What Do You Think?' questions in this book, it is important that you not only state your opinion but also give as many reasons as possible for your opinion.

1. The Dalai Lama drew strength from the Buddha's teachings. What would you do to give yourself courage?

A Compassionate Being

Buddhists believe that people have all had millions of lives. If people's minds contain greed, hatred and ignorance they will suffer, and cause others to suffer. In addition they can expect to face the consequences of this in their next life. Buddhists are encouraged to think carefully about this and investigate what it means through meditation.

Buddhists reason that if people have all lived through many lifetimes, then everyone (and every creature) has at some point in the past been everyone else's best friend or parent and has been very kind or sacrificed their happiness for them. Thus everyone should be grateful to all people and all creatures and treat them with compassion, or loving-kindness. Buddhists try to free themselves from hatred, greed and ignorance so that they will reach Enlightenment and will not need to be reborn ever again into a body which will suffer and die. Tibetan Buddhists believe that some people who become so wise and kind that they do not need to be reborn choose out of compassion to do so in order to help human beings. These people are known as 'bodhisattvas' and can choose where they will be reborn. Tibetans believe there are many buddhas (perfectly wise and compassionate beings) and bodhisattvas (buddhas-to-be). When they are reincarnated (reborn) as humans, Tibetans call them 'tulkus'. Children believed to be tulkus are born every year, but the most important is the Dalai Lama.

The 14th Dalai Lama as a young child

Tibetans regard him as both their political and their religious leader. His authority is wide sweeping and unquestioned, and he is seen by most Tibetans as a real and living buddha.

Tibetan Buddhists believe that the Dalai Lama is an incarnation (human form) of the buddha who represents perfect love and compassion, called Chenrezig. They often explain how a buddha can be everywhere and yet a particular person at the same time as like the way the moon is always up in the sky, but we can see an image of it reflected on a still lake. In the same way, the Buddha Chenrezig always exists even though we can see a human form of him here on Earth.

What Do You Think?

1. Buddhism teaches that people suffer when their minds are filled with greed and hatred. Give some examples to explain how this can happen.

2. Buddhism also teaches that by thinking kind and friendly thoughts about others, people can be happier themselves. Can you think of times when this has been true for you?

Finding the 14th Dalai Lama

When the Dalai Lama dies he is reincarnated (born again in a new human form) as the next Dalai Lama. In 1937 a boy who had only just turned two, Lhamo Thondup, was identified by senior monks as the reincarnation of and successor to the 13th Dalai Lama, who had died in 1933.

Immediately after the 13th Dalai Lama died curious cloud formations appeared over the north-east of Lhasa and a strange fungus grew on the north-eastern pillar of the room in the city where his body lay. A few days later his head had turned in the same direction. It seemed that his spirit was giving a sign that the next incarnation of the Dalai Lama was to be born in the north-east of the country.

The most senior monk in Tibet travelled to a sacred lake, where he saw a vision of a monastery by a hill. Across from the hill the vision showed an unusual house with an oddly shaped gutter, and a brown and white dog. The monk sent out search parties to locate the house in the vision and eventually one group reported just such a place over a thousand miles away.

A party of senior monks and officials set out to see if this place was indeed the home of the next (14th) Dalai Lama. They were disguised as merchants with the leader of the group, the abbot of the main monastery in Lhasa, pretending to be a servant.

They found the monastery by the hill, the house and even the dog just as reported. While the main party were chatting with the husband and wife of the house and drinking tea, the abbot went for a look around the farm. Outside the kitchen a little boy, their son Lhamo, came running up to him and jumped into his lap. He grabbed a string of prayer-beads from around the 'servant's' neck and said, 'This is mine, this is mine, why do you have it?' The beads had belonged to the previous Dalai Lama. Lhamo also spoke in the accent of a person from Lhasa, very different to his parents and everyone else in this remote region.

The abbot was not sure he had found the right child so the party went back to Lhasa to prepare more tests.

When they returned to Lhamo's home, they set out before him a number of objects which had belonged to the 13th Dalai Lama, together with more attractive but fake versions of the same items. In every case the boy chose the 'correct' item, claiming it was really his. He had some trouble choosing between two walking-sticks, but it was discovered later that they had both belonged to the previous Dalai Lama. However he had given one of them away soon after obtaining it. There was no longer any doubt – this young boy was the reincarnation of the 13th Dalai Lama!

What Do You Think?

1. How convincing do you find the evidence which led to the discovery of Lhamo? How important are dreams and visions for some religious people?

Growing Up in the Potala

In a grand ceremony Lhamo was given a new name, Tenzin Gyatso, and the title 'Dalai Lama', which means 'Ocean of Wisdom'. ('Lama' is the Tibetan word for a wise religious teacher. 'Dalai' means 'ocean'.) People who were present at the ceremony remember the incredible calmness and patience of the young boy, who blessed people and sat listening to prayers, chants and meditations for hour after hour without complaining or fidgeting.

His parents attended this ceremony and stayed with him for a full year through all the procedures for making him officially the 14th Dalai Lama, but finally they had to return to their farm hundreds of miles away.

The Potala Palace photographed from the Chakpori medical school in Lhasa in 1937

6

The Dalai Lama was taken to his official winter residence, the Potala Palace in Lhasa, which he found large, cold and gloomy. The Potala was both a palace and a monastery housing around 175 monks as well as many government officials. There he was placed on the Lion Throne, an enormous, beautifully carved, jewel-encrusted throne which no one except the Dalai Lama may use. He usually had no family, friends or playmates of his own age to keep him company apart from his elder brother Lobsang. His other companions, guardians and teachers were all monks or middle-aged servants who swept and cleaned the monastery. They were mostly very kind and played with the boys all the time.

The Dalai Lama was being trained for a very important job: to be the leader and senior religious guide for all Tibetans. First he was accepted as a novice monk. His head was shaved and he was given maroon monk's robes to wear. Then his education began. He and Lobsang were taught to read and he vividly remembers his schoolrooms. On the walls hung a silk whip and a leather whip – the first one was reserved for the Dalai Lama and the second for his brother! The whips terrified both of them. Although the silk one never needed to be used, Lobsang was not a great student and did suffer a few lashes from the leather whip.

The Dalai Lama would wait for his brother to finish his lessons so that they could go and play. This usually involved races and hide-and-seek, when they could disappear for hours on end and send the elderly monks into a panic. There were endless amounts of brotherly scrapping. Lobsang recalls, 'One of us would poke the other, or say something, and it would go on from there.'

However when Lobsang reached eight years old he was sent away to school and the brothers saw each other just once a month. The Dalai Lama's mother was able to visit only very occasionally, and although he saw his father more often, he died when the boy was twelve.

The Dalai Lama remembers how, as a child, he used to watch the prisoners in the city jail through a telescope. From his window high up on the seventh floor of the palace, he could see them pacing up and down in the yard and almost felt jealous of their freedom. He always knew when one was released and when a new prisoner arrived. He thought of them as his friends even though he never spoke to them. He even enjoyed the company of the mice which ran about his room and over his bed as he lay in it!

His daily routine usually began at around 6 a.m. with an hour's prayer and meditation followed by breakfast. He spent the rest of the morning and afternoon until around half past five studying, apart from a break when he sat in on government meetings, followed by an hour's playtime before lunch. He had to attend government meetings from a very young age as part of his training for the time when he would take over leadership of the nation. In lessons he studied the scriptures and rituals of Buddhism, Buddhist philosophy, Sanskrit (the language many Buddhist scriptures are written in), Tibetan art and culture, medicine, music and drama.

Amongst the Dalai Lama's favourite toys were a clockwork train set and a box of Meccano. He has always enjoyed taking things to bits and seeing how they work. He did this with his mechanical toys and even today his hobbies include repairing watches, cameras and other machines. He says that this helps him understand Buddhist teachings, because they involve studying how the mind works through investigating it in great detail and improving it.

He was an excellent student, although he claims to have been a 'reluctant pupil' who 'disliked all subjects equally'! All his exams were oral, in the form of debates. This meant that he had to memorize enormous amounts of the scriptures and use them to win arguments.

The method of debating used by Tibetans is quite remarkable. They do not sit calmly in chairs and discuss

issues. One person sits on the floor and makes a statement, then another person walks around him hurling questions whilst waving and clapping his hands and stamping his feet to upset his opponent's concentration. When a debate really gets exciting some of the audience (who are already cheering and making a racket) might jump up and join in. It is all good natured, but rather intimidating. You can be sure that any gaps in the debater's knowledge or understanding will be exposed very publicly! The Dalai Lama was not given an easy ride just because of who he was. By succeeding in his education he became an excellent debater and philosopher.

What Do You Think?

1. The Dalai Lama had a highly unusual childhood, and he says he was sometimes lonely. How do you think his upbringing *helped* him become wise and compassionate in later life?

2. How do you think meditation in the morning might help to prepare a person to face the day?

The Dalai Lama and Animals

One of the most important lessons a Buddhist learns is that people should have compassion for all living beings – animals as well as humans. This came quite naturally to the Dalai Lama. When he used to see farmers passing his window in Lhasa taking yaks to the market he would often send one of his assistants out to buy the animals to save them from being slaughtered. He reckons that he saved over ten thousand animals in this way.

He learnt from his mistakes too. One of his assistants had a parrot which used to take nuts from his hand whilst having its head stroked. The Dalai Lama also wished to be friends with the bird but did not have the patience to win it over, so one day he threatened it with a stick. Needless to say, after that it fled whenever it saw him. He later wrote, 'This was a very good lesson in how to make friends: not by force but by compassion.'

The Dalai Lama has also had curious experiences with cats. He came home once to find Tsering the cat killing a mouse. He shouted at her and in fright she ran to the top of a curtain, fell and was so badly injured that she died. Not long afterwards he found a small kitten which had her legs damaged in the exact places where Tsering had been fatally wounded. She spent her whole life with him but he decided not to have a pet again after she died. Then in 1988 he found a sick kitten outside his kitchens. To his utter amazement she was crippled in just the same way, so she now lives with him.

What Do You Think?

1. Why do you think the Dalai Lama did not simply order the farmers to release their yaks?

2. What did the Dalai Lama learn from his experience with the parrot? Do you think you can make a true friend by forcing someone to like you?

Tibet

Despite being the size of western Europe, in the 1940s Tibet had a population of just six million. The people were not interested in building an empire or seeking major trading deals with other countries. Almost all the population were hard-working farmers, growing all their food and keeping just enough livestock for themselves and their families to survive on. Tibet had a tiny, untrained army and had not joined the United Nations. The 13th Dalai Lama was one of the very few Tibetans who foresaw how the world was changing in the twentieth century and how Tibet could not remain totally isolated, but no one really listened to him.

In 1949 the Chinese Communist Party took control of China. The Tibetans did not realize at first what that meant for their country. The Communist government tried to convince the Chinese people that Tibetans were very unhappy and desperately wanted to be saved from their rulers. They claimed that Chinese soldiers would be sent to Tibet to help the people but would leave as soon as they were asked to do so.

In October 1950 the eastern region of Tibet was invaded by 80 000 Chinese troops. The Chinese government wanted the wealth of Tibet's natural resources and huge land area, which increased China's size by more than one third. The Dalai Lama sent messages to the USA, Britain, India, Nepal and the United Nations asking for help. He was shocked when the world agreed to express disapproval of the Chinese invasion but would not help Tibet.

In the meantime the Tibetan government had decided that in the current crisis the Dalai Lama should be given full responsibility for running the country, but he did not feel he was mature enough. Nevertheless in November, the Dalai Lama recalls,

'I found myself undisputed leader of six million people facing the threat of full-scale war. And I was still only fifteen years old. It was an impossible situation to be in, but I saw it as my duty to avoid this disaster if at all possible.'

One of the Dalai Lama's first tasks as leader was to meet a Chinese general who had brought an 'agreement' from his government for him to sign. The Dalai Lama had to agree that Tibet was really part of China, and in return China would promise not to interfere with the Tibetans' religion, culture, education, agriculture or any other aspect of their life.

The agreement also specifically said that Chinese soldiers in Tibet would treat the people well and buy food from them fairly. The young Dalai Lama realized that without any support from other countries he had little choice but to sign. Although Tibet would lose its independence, he felt hopeful that his people would be able to live their lives peacefully.

Within weeks, thousands of Chinese troops had moved into Lhasa. Many took over buildings, forced the Tibetans onto the streets and took their food supplies. Famine broke out – the first in Lhasa for over a thousand years. The Chinese authorities forced Tibetan farmers to grow different crops, more suited to the lowland Chinese climate. The harvests were very poor, and hunger became widespread. Hundreds of thousands of Tibetans starved to death.

The agreement was broken in other ways too. The colourful material Tibetans used for their clothing

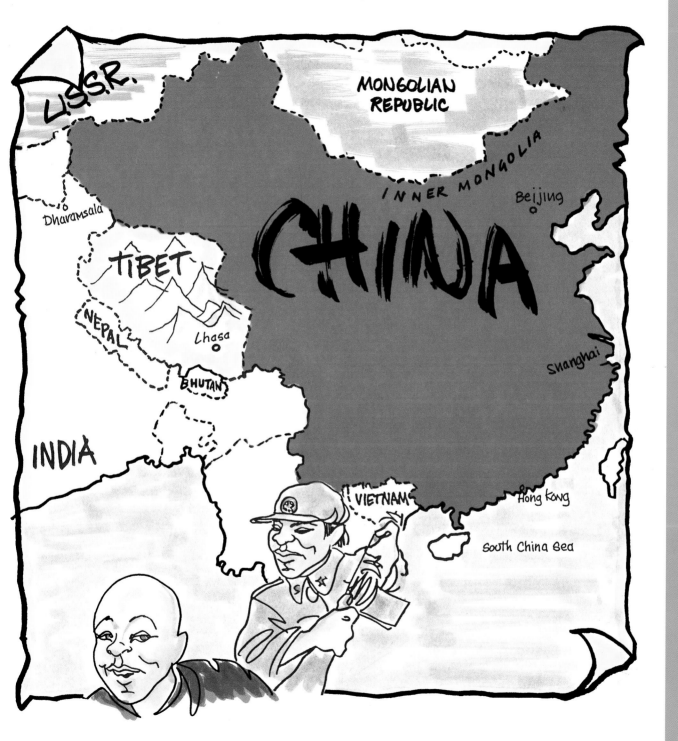

suddenly became 'unavailable'. The only clothes they could buy were Communist-style Chinese jackets, which were drab and identical. In schools all lessons now had to be in Chinese, and children were taught that they should reject everything Tibetan. Many parents preferred to keep their children at home and since then the standard of education in Tibet has been in decline.

A Tibetan woman wearing traditional clothes and jewellery

What Do You Think?

1. Tibet was a poor country by Western standards. Why do you think most Tibetans had no great desire to change their way of life?

2. Powerful countries are sometimes quick to help a smaller country when it is in trouble. Why do you think powerful countries help some smaller countries, but not others?

3. The Dalai Lama found himself running a country at the age of fifteen. What qualities do you think a teenager would need to do this?

4. Why did the Chinese invasion lead to widespread starvation amongst Tibetans for the first time?

5. Why do you think the Chinese have been trying to force the Tibetans to change their way of life?

Tension Grows

In 1954, the Dalai Lama was invited to Beijing, the capital of China, to meet its leader, Chairman Mao. Mao was the man who had ordered the invasion of Tibet and was responsible for all that had happened. Mao was very polite to the Dalai Lama. Probably he thought that he could easily impress this young man and convince him that China had Tibet's best interests at heart.

The Dalai Lama spent many months in China learning about the country, although he was never allowed to talk to any ordinary Chinese people. He was actually quite impressed by Chairman Mao until at the end of their last meeting Mao stunned him with the remark, 'Religion is poison.' The Dalai Lama immediately responded, 'You are the destroyer of the Dharma after all!' (The Dharma is the teachings of the Buddha.)

Soon after returning to Tibet, the Dalai Lama began learning of further suffering inflicted on his people. His letters to Chairman Mao complaining of the terrible treatment of Tibetan people were constantly ignored and he realized that the Chinese leader had been trying to fool him all along. The Dalai Lama was shocked to see a photograph in a Chinese newspaper of a row of severed heads which belonged to Tibetans who had tried to resist the Chinese.

Non-violence is an important part of the Buddhist religion. However, in 1956, a number of Tibetans decided that in such desperate circumstances it was morally right to start fighting for independence – to save their country. A small group of freedom-fighters was formed. Despite the pleas of the Dalai Lama to avoid violence, more and more Tibetans were driven to join the resistance or support it. The Chinese response was swift and brutal. The Dalai Lama felt that the resistance fighters' attempts to defeat the Chinese were never going to be successful, but he admired their courage

and accepted that they had been driven to such measures in desperation, often after seeing their families massacred.

Early in 1959 the Dalai Lama completed his final monastic exams. Shortly after, by the beginning of March, it was clear that the patience of those Tibetans who had held back so far was about to give way. Over a hundred thousand tense and angry Tibetans were crammed into Lhasa. They had long-term and harsh experience of the behaviour of the Chinese occupying forces. It was clear that they could no longer tolerate the suffering without trying to do something.

The crisis came when, on 10 March, the Dalai Lama was ordered by the Chinese military to attend a dance show. The crowds of Tibetans in Lhasa suspected that the Chinese intended to kidnap the Dalai Lama and surrounded his palace to protect him. The Chinese general was furious about the crowds and ordered the Tibetans to remove the barricades they had put up.

To avoid deaths, the Dalai Lama would have given himself to the Chinese, but as Tibetans have often said, 'His Holiness is the figurehead; he is Tibet. As long as he lives the Tibetan people have a focus.' The people would rather have lost their lives than lose the Dalai Lama.

On 16 March 1959, the Chinese general broke the tense waiting by declaring he would shell the Potala Palace and attack the crowd. The Dalai Lama was left with no choice. The next night he fled to India. Once news had reached his people of his successful escape, thousands of Tibetans followed him into exile.

What Do You Think?

1. Mao said, 'Religion is poison.' Why might someone believe this? What is your view?

2. How far do you think Mao's statement, 'Religion is poison', explains the difference in behaviour between the Dalai Lama and the Chinese leaders?

3. Why do you think many Tibetans would rather have died than lose the Dalai Lama?

The Dalai Lama and his companions escaping to India in March 1959

Refugees

The Prime Minister of India, Mr Nehru, sent a telegram welcoming the Dalai Lama's escape party. Within days news reporters arrived from all over the world. The Chinese government said that the protests in Lhasa had been organized against the will of the people and that the Dalai Lama had really been kidnapped by rebels. India was already taking a risk by harbouring the Tibetan refugees and needed to keep relations with China friendly. The Dalai Lama began to realize that Tibet's future was by no means bright. He was bitterly disappointed.

Two months after his dramatic escape, the Dalai Lama held an international press conference to tackle the propaganda being spread by the Chinese government. The Indian government refused to recognize his Tibetan government in exile but still welcomed all the refugees and let him voice his views freely.

The Dalai Lama lost tremendous wealth by fleeing his palaces and monasteries in Tibet. Now he found himself in the unusual position for a Dalai Lama of being able to experience at first hand the Buddhist teaching that wealth could not bring true and lasting happiness.

In April 1960, the Dalai Lama and his staff moved to Dharamsala in Northern India. Within a fortnight he had opened the first nursery for refugee children.

The Indian Prime Minister made it clear that he believed that the refugee children were most important. They should continue to be educated in the Tibetan way, funded by the Indian government. He also said that they must be taught about the modern world and learn the English language, as that would be a great help to them in the outside world. The Dalai Lama was delighted. He had been trying to drag certain aspects of Tibetan life into the twentieth century for two lifetimes!

The Dalai Lama believed Tibetan refugees should not forget their past, but try to rebuild the Tibetan community in exile. Religion deeply affects every aspect of Tibetan life, even more deeply than a desire for money and possessions affect modern western society. The Dalai Lama decided there was no reason why his religion should not survive, so he had new monasteries built for monks and nuns who had fled Tibet. Today there is a thriving monastic community of more than six thousand.

Escaping refugees have brought religious hangings, books and relics to save them from Chinese destruction. They presented these to the Dalai Lama, who in turn handed them to the Library of Tibetan Works and Archives at Dharamsala. The Library now has more than 40 000 original Tibetan books.

Today at least 120 000 Tibetans live in exile. The communities they have established in India are strong and successful. The Dalai Lama says that if it had not been for the generosity of the government and people of India in providing the money, land and support for a community in exile, then the culture, religion and national identity of the people of Tibet would by now have been destroyed.

What Do You Think?

1. Should other countries help Tibetan refugees? If so, how could they best do that? How can individuals help?

2. The Dalai Lama would like refugees who have completed their education in India to go back to Tibet, despite the dangers. Why do you think he wants this?

World Statesman

The Dalai Lama has met many world-famous political and religious leaders. He welcomes them all to Dharamsala as well as the homeless, sick and destitute. Those who meet him leave with a sense of his profound warmth, humour and wisdom.

Since 1959, the Chinese government has flooded Tibet with Chinese immigrants, so that there are now more Chinese people than Tibetans in Tibet. These immigrants have been given the best land and favourable treatment. Tibetans are always very careful to distinguish between the Chinese authorities and ordinary Chinese people who have no more freedom to disagree with their rulers than the Tibetans do. Although Tibetans can be shot dead for nothing more than having a Tibetan flag, they do not take out their frustration and pain on the Chinese immigrants.

This is because the Dalai Lama preaches very clearly against the use of violence. Tibetans have followed his teachings for more than half a century, but there is a fear that after he dies many younger Tibetans could lose their faith in his patient non-violent principles and the most terrible bloodshed could result.

The Dalai Lama's policy of non-violence has sound reasoning behind it. He says, 'Non-violence is for us the only way. Quite patently in our case violence would be tantamount to suicide. For this reason, whether we like

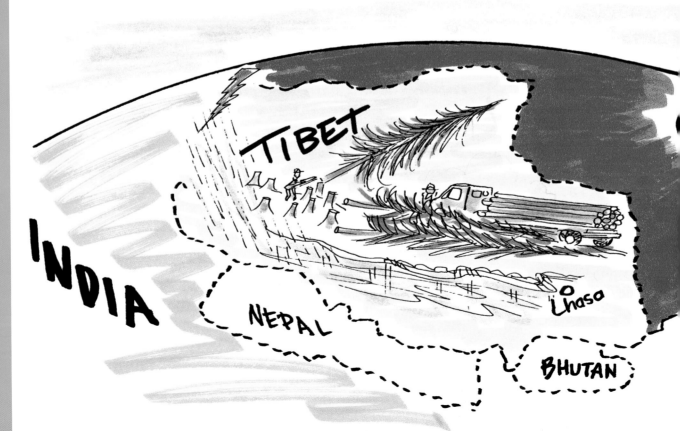

it or not, non-violence is the only approach, and the right one. We only need more patience and determination.'

In 1987, the Dalai Lama proposed that Tibet should be made into a 'peace zone', an area with no army or weapons where the rights of Tibetan people would be protected. There should be proper talks and plans drawn up for the future of Tibet with the agreement of both its Tibetan and its Chinese population. However, China should stop sending huge numbers of immigrants to Tibet.

The Dalai Lama's peace plan also contains measures to conserve Tibet's natural environment. The Chinese authorities have cut down huge areas of forest in Tibet. This has led to soil being washed away into Tibet's major rivers and disastrous flooding far downstream in India and Bangladesh.

The destruction of Tibet's forests is also one of the causes of the extinction of much of its wildlife. The Dalai Lama said, 'Tibetan people regard life, any life, as something very sacred, something holy and important, so even when a small insect is killed, we immediately respond with some feeling of compassion. This remains a force in our society.'

He also said, 'Our planet is our house, and we must keep it in order and take care of it if we are genuinely concerned about happiness for ourselves, our children, our friends, and other beings who share this great house with us.' Before the Chinese invasion, Tibetans could not have imagined a need for nature reserves,

because they see the Earth as a beautiful whole.

China rejected all the Dalai Lama's proposals and when Tibetans carried out peaceful protests, Chinese soldiers opened fire on them. Most governments across the world remain cautious and give more importance to doing business with China than challenging the Chinese occupation of Tibet and their abuse of human rights.

In 1996 it became a crime in Tibet even to carry any pictures of the Dalai Lama. People protest against this by placing an empty photograph frame on display to show the love and devotion which they still hold for their exiled leader.

What Do You Think?

1. Explain how damage caused to the environment in one country can cause disasters in other countries. How far should one country consider the effects of its actions on other parts of the world?

2. Should people be concerned about the damage to the land, trees and rivers of Tibet when so many people living there are suffering?

The Nobel Peace Prize

The Dalai Lama's restraint in never having given in to hate is truly profound. He personally greets all Tibetan refugees on their arrival at Dharamsala and listens to their tales of loss, pain and anguish through their tears.

Day after day he sees orphaned children, torture victims, abused nuns, homeless and frightened people in a constant flow of suffering. Somehow he turns that pain into a positive and strong community in exile.

In 1989 he was awarded the Nobel Peace Prize for his consistent resistance to the use of violence in his people's struggle for freedom and independence. In his acceptance speech, he said:

'What is the purpose of life for a human being? I believe that happiness is the purpose of life. Whether or not there is a purpose to the existence of the universe or galaxies, I don't know. In any case, the fact is that we are here on this planet with other human beings. Then, since every human being wants happiness and does not want suffering, it is clear that this desire does not come from training, or from some ideology. It is something natural. Therefore, I consider that the attainment of happiness, peace, and joy is the purpose of life. Therefore, it is very important to investigate what are happiness and satisfaction and what are their causes.

'What is my purpose in life, what is my responsibility? Whether I like it or not, I am on this planet, and it is far better to do something for humanity. So you see that compassion is the seed or basis. If we take care to foster compassion, we will see that it brings the other good human qualities. The topic of compassion is not at all religious business; it is very important to know that it is human business, that is a question of human survival, that is not a question of human luxury. I might say that religion is a kind of luxury. If you have religion, that is good. But it is clear that even without religion we can manage. However, without these basic human qualities we cannot survive. It is a question of our own peace and mental stability.

'Now, on the question of violence and non-violence. There are many different levels of violence and non-violence. On the basis of external action, it is difficult to distinguish whether an action is violent or non-violent. Basically, it depends on the motivation behind the action. If the motivation is negative, even though the external appearance may be very smooth and gentle, in a deeper sense the action is very violent. On the contrary, harsh actions and words done with a sincere, positive motivation are essentially non-violent. In other words, violence is a destructive power. Non-violence is constructive.

'Practically speaking, through violence we may achieve something, but at the expense of someone else's welfare. That way, although we may solve one problem, we simultaneously seed a new problem. The best way to solve problems is through human understanding, mutual respect. On one side make some concessions; on the other side take serious consideration about the problem. There may not be complete satisfaction, but something happens, at least future danger is avoided. Non-violence is very safe.

'If there are sound reasons or bases for the points you demand, then there is no need to use violence. On the other hand, when there is no sound reason that concessions should be made to you but mainly your own desire, then reason cannot work and you have to rely on force. Thus using force is not a sign of strength but rather a sign of weakness. Even in daily human contact, if we talk seriously, using reasons, there is no need to feel anger. We can argue the points. When we fail to prove with reason, then anger comes. When reason ends, then anger begins. Therefore, anger is a sign of weakness.

'As a Buddhist monk, and as a result of more contact with people from other traditions, as time passes I have firmed my conviction that all religions can work together despite fundamental difference in philosophy. Every religion aims at serving humanity. Therefore, it is possible for the various religions to work together to serve humanity and contribute to world peace. So during these last few years, at every opportunity I try to develop closer relations with other religions.'

When questioned on his feelings towards the Chinese occupiers of Tibet, the Dalai Lama says he 'almost never' hates them. When he does it is only for a moment – his compassion for them returns soon after. The Dalai Lama has always thought of himself as 'a simple Buddhist monk' and humbly regards that as his greatest status and most important job. It is his dream that Tibet will become an independent country once more. Then he will be able to withdraw and focus on private study and meditation, and his own spiritual journey.

What Do You Think?

1. If everyone wants 'happiness, peace and joy', why do you think there is so much misery and conflict in the world?

2. How far do you agree that the human race cannot survive without compassion?

3. How far do you agree with the Dalai Lama's views on religion? Would you expect such an argument from a major religious leader?

4. Explain what you understand by the different levels of violence and non-violence the Dalai Lama talks about.

5. How far do you agree that 'anger is a sign of weakness'?

6. Do you think people of different religions can or should work together? Give reasons for your views.

Biographical Notes

1933	Death of the 13th Dalai Lama, spiritual leader of Tibet.
1937	Two-year-old Lhamo Thondup is identified by senior Buddhist holy men as the 14th Dalai Lama.
1938	The 14th Dalai Lama is taken to the Potala Palace in Lhasa and becomes a novice monk.
1949	Chairman Mao's Communist Party takes control of China.
1950	80 000 Chinese troops invade Tibet. The fifteen-year-old Dalai Lama is immediately made official leader of Tibet.
1954	The Dalai Lama is invited to Beijing to meet Mao. He spends more than a year in China.
1956	The Buddhist principle of non-violence is set aside by Tibetan freedom-fighters in their desperation at Chinese brutality, torture, intimidation and mass killing.
Early 1959	The Dalai Lama completes his final monastic exams as tension grows between Tibetans and the occupying Chinese.
March 1959	The crisis breaks and the Dalai Lama has to flee from Lhasa in a daring night-time escape. He and his party cross the treacherous heights and survive the cold of the Himalayas to reach India.
April 1960	Prime Minister Nehru of India gives the refugees who followed the Dalai Lama into exile a site for a Tibetan community at Dharamsala. Today the refugee population there is 120 000. The Chinese meanwhile begin flooding Tibet with Chinese immigrants.
1987	The Dalai Lama writes a peace plan which aims to make Tibet into a peace zone with no military bases, soldiers or weapons belonging to any nation. He also proposes measures for environmental protection.
1989	The Dalai Lama is awarded the Nobel Peace Prize.
1996	Pictures and photographs of the Dalai Lama are banned by the Chinese occupiers of Tibet. Repression continues in Tibet on a destructive scale with the steady elimination of Tibetan culture by the Chinese.

Things to Do

1 Produce a collage or cartoon strip on the Dalai Lama's escape into exile.

2 Compare the Dalai Lama's daily schedule as a schoolchild with your own. Illustrate the differences in a collage or cartoon strip, and describe the main differences.

3 Tibetan debates are most unusual and entertaining. One person tries to defend an argument whilst another attempts to disprove it. However, the person defending the argument can reply using only four statements. They are:

- I agree.
- Why? Give me a reason.
- It does not follow.
- We have not proved your last reason yet.

See if you can debate with a partner using these rules. You could start with one of the following statements, or try your own:

(a) We should not eat animals.

(b) Non-violence just produces losers.

4 Some Tibetan children are 'sponsored' by Westerners. Imagine you have just escaped from Tibet and have arrived in Dharamsala. Write a letter to your sponsor describing your experiences and hopes.

5 Do some research to find out more about one or more of the following:

(a) Charities, sponsorships and events to help Tibetans

(b) Famous musicians and film stars who support the Tibetan cause

(c) Tibetan Buddhist groups in Britain

(d) The 'Cultural Revolution' in China

(e) The situation in Tibet today

Present your findings in an illustrated booklet.

6 Find out about the work of Amnesty International and their campaigns to help Tibetan prisoners, including a group of nuns given long prison sentences for singing songs about Tibet in Lhasa. Make an eye-catching poster with a good slogan to portray one of the campaigns.

7 This is a common Buddhist meditation you could try. It is not really 'religious' and can be attempted by someone of any religion or none. It is called 'A Meditation on Friendliness':

(a) Sit comfortably, either cross-legged on a cushion on the floor, or sit on a chair. Make sure your back is straight and your eyes are lightly closed. Breathe gently for a few moments until you feel relaxed.

(b) When you are ready, picture in your mind a photograph or image of yourself. Silently say to yourself, 'May I be happy, may I be well, may everything go well for me.' Repeat this to yourself for about 2 minutes. If it helps, you could imagine a warm ball of light glowing in your heart as you say this.

(c) After about 2 minutes, picture a close friend in front of you. Repeat silently the phrase 'May *you* be well, may *you* be happy, may everything go well for *you*' to him or her for the same amount of time. If it helps, you could imagine yourself giving them a gift as you say this.

(d) When you are ready to move on, imagine a neutral person – in other words, someone you see around but do not know very well, and have no feelings about either way. It could be someone on the bus you have never spoken to or someone in another class you hardly know. Picture them and repeat silently the same phrase to them as you did with your friend.

(e) Next, when you are ready, picture in your mind someone you really dislike or who has upset you recently. Now say silently to that person for 2 minutes, 'May you be well, may you be happy, may everything go well for you.'

(f) Finally, try to imagine yourself and the other three people in your meditation standing next to each other, smiling. Develop a feeling of equal liking for all of them. Now gradually 'pan out' to include all the people around you, all the people in your neighbourhood, in your country, in all the world, together with all the animals, and wish them the same as you wished the people at the start of your meditation.

(g) When you have tried to develop feelings of peace and happiness for the whole world, rest your mind for a short while. When you feel ready, gradually open your eyes and remain at rest for as long as you wish.

Try this meditation, or read it carefully if you do not want to do it yourself. Afterwards, think about or discuss what benefits this meditation might have. Think of different possible benefits, both immediate and longer term, for both the person meditating and the subjects of the meditation.

8 Find out about other Buddhist meditation practices. Explain the different ways you think they can help a person train their mind to become more calm, patient and loving.

9 As a group role-playing exercise, imagine fifty Tibetan refugees have been given permission to settle in your community. They have no possessions and do not speak English. How could your community help? Why might some people object?

Take on the roles of different members of the community to discuss this proposal.

Questions for Assessment or Examination Candidates

10 (a) Describe and explain the Buddhist beliefs about karma (or kamma), rebirth (or reincarnation) and Enlightenment. (8 marks)

(b) How might these teachings help a Buddhist develop compassion? (7 marks)

(c) 'You don't need to believe in life after death to be a good person.' Do you agree? Give reasons to support your answer and show that you have thought about different points of view. You must refer to religious beliefs in your answer. (5 marks)

11 (a) Describe and explain Buddhist attitudes towards the natural world. (8 marks)

(b) How might these attitudes cause problems for a Buddhist in Britain? (7 marks)

(c) 'Vegetarians shouldn't impose their views on others.' Do you agree? Give reasons to support your answer and show that you have thought about different points of view. You must refer to religious beliefs in your answer. (5 marks)

12 (a) Describe and explain Buddhist attitudes towards violence. (8 marks)

(b) Explain how the Dalai Lama has put Buddhist principles of non-violence and compassion into practice. (7 marks)

(c) 'Sometimes violence is the only way to solve problems.' Do you agree? Give reasons to support your answer and show that you have thought about different points of view. You must refer to religious beliefs in your answer. (5 marks)

Religious and Moral Education Press
A division of SCM-Canterbury Press Ltd,
a subsidiary of
Hymns Ancient & Modern Ltd
St Mary's Works, St Mary's Plain
Norwich, Norfolk NR3 3BH

First published 1997
Reprinted 2002

ISBN 1 85175 121 1

Designed and typeset by
TOPICS – The Creative Partnership,
Exeter

Printed in Great Britain by
Brightsea Press, Exeter for
Religious and Moral Education Press,
Norwich

Notes for Teachers

The first Faith in Action books were published in the late 1970s and the series has remained popular with both teachers and pupils. However, much in education has changed over the last twenty years, such as the development of both new examination syllabuses in Religious Studies and local agreed syllabuses for Religious Education which place more emphasis on pupils' own understanding, interpretation and evaluation of religious belief and practice, rather than a simple knowledge of events. This has encouraged us to amend the style of the Faith in Action Series to make it more suitable for today's classroom.

The aim is, as before, to tell the stories of people who have lived and acted according to their faith, but we have included alongside the main story questions which will encourage pupils to think about the reasons for the behaviour of our main characters and to empathize with the situations in which they found themselves. We hope that pupils will also be able to relate some of the issues in the stories to other issues in modern society, either in their own area or on a global scale.

The 'What Do You Think?' questions may be used for group or class discussion or for short written exercises. The 'Things to Do' at the end of the story include ideas for longer activities and more-structured questions suitable for assessment or examination practice.

In line with current syllabus requirements, as Britain is a multifaith society, Faith in Action characters will be selected from a wide variety of faith backgrounds and many of the questions may be answered from the perspective of more than one faith.

CMB, 1997

Acknowledgements
The publishers would like to thank Tibet Images for providing the photographs reproduced in this book: cover – Chris Langridge; page 4 – Tibet Images; page 6 – Pitt Rivers Museum/Spencer Chapman Archive; page 12 – Paloma Brinkman; page 14 – D.I.I.R. Dharamsala.